RANDY'S CORNER

DAY BY DAY WITH...

ALEX MORGAN

BY
JOHN TORRES

Mitchell Lane
PUBLISHERS

P.O. Box 196
Hockessin, Delaware 19707
Visit us on the web: www.mitchelllane.com
Comments? Email us:
mitchelllane@mitchelllane.com

Printing   1   2   3   4   5   6   7   8   9

RANDY'S CORNER

DAY BY DAY WITH. . .

Alex Morgan	Manny Machado
Beyoncé	Mia Hamm
Bindi Sue Irwin	Miley Cyrus
Chloë Moretz	Missy Franklin
Dwayne "The Rock" Johnson	Selena Gomez
Eli Manning	Shaun White
Gabby Douglas	Stephen Hillenburg
Justin Bieber	Taylor Swift
LeBron James	Willow Smith

Library of Congress Cataloging-in-Publication Data
Torres, John Albert.
 Day by day with Alex Morgan / by John A. Torres.
    pages cm. — (Randy's corner)
 Includes bibliographical references and index.
 ISBN 978-1-61228-452-1 (library bound)
 1. Morgan, Alex (Alexandra Patricia), 1989– —Juvenile literature. 2. Women soccer players—United States—Biography—Juvenile literature. I. Title.
 GV942.7.M673T67 2014
 796.334092—dc23
 [B]
                                                                                                2013023042
eBook ISBN: 9781612285115

ABOUT THE AUTHOR: John A. Torres is an award-winning sports columnist for *Florida Today* newspaper where he has covered professional and collegiate sports. John also covered the 2006 Olympics and has reported from many countries around the world. John is the author of more than 50 books, the majority of them about sports.

PUBLISHER'S NOTE: The following story has been thoroughly researched and to the best of our knowledge represents a true story. While every possible effort has been made to ensure accuracy, the publisher will not assume liability for damages caused by inaccuracies in the data and makes no warranty on the accuracy of the information contained herein. This story has not been authorized or endorsed by Alex Morgan.

PLB

DAY BY DAY WITH **ALEX MORGAN**

Alex Morgan is one of the best soccer players in the world. Recently, she has also become one of the most popular athletes.

Alex appears in fashion magazines and attends parties with lots of famous people. By the time she was 23 years old, she had already played in the World Cup and won an Olympic gold medal.

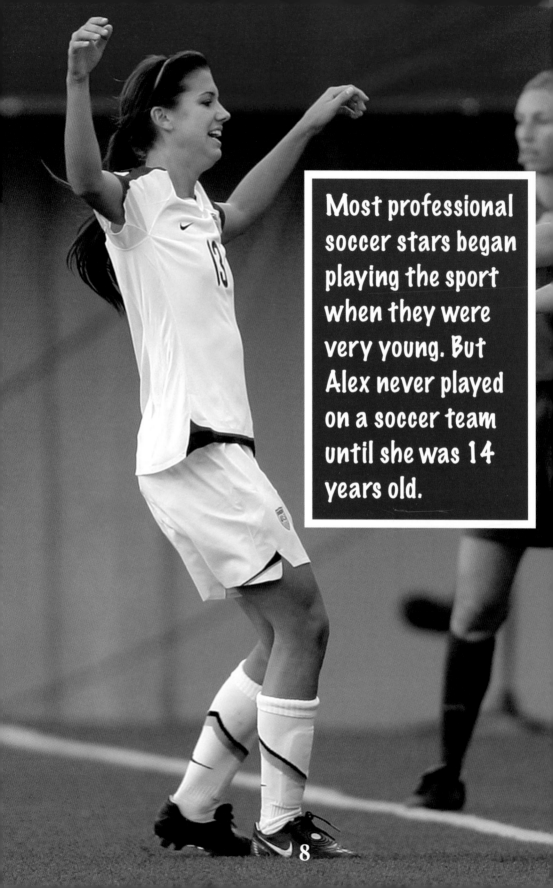

Most professional soccer stars began playing the sport when they were very young. But Alex never played on a soccer team until she was 14 years old.

ALEX MORGAN, LEFT, CELEBRATES WITH TEAMMATES AFTER SCORING DURING THE WOMEN'S UNDER-20 WORLD CUP. THE FINAL GAME WAS PLAYED AGAINST NORTH KOREA IN SANTIAGO, CHILE.

It didn't take long for Alex to show everyone that she was a special kind of player.

She was the fastest runner on the soccer field and scored a lot of goals on breakaways. She would simply outrun everyone else.

ALEX WAS SO FAST THAT HER TEAMMATES CALLED HER "BABY HORSE."

Alexandra Patricia Morgan was born on July 2, 1989, to parents Michael and Pamela. She and her two older sisters Jennifer and Jeri grew up in a town called Diamond Bar, California. Alex joined the soccer team at Diamond Bar High School. She quickly became the best player on the team and in the league.

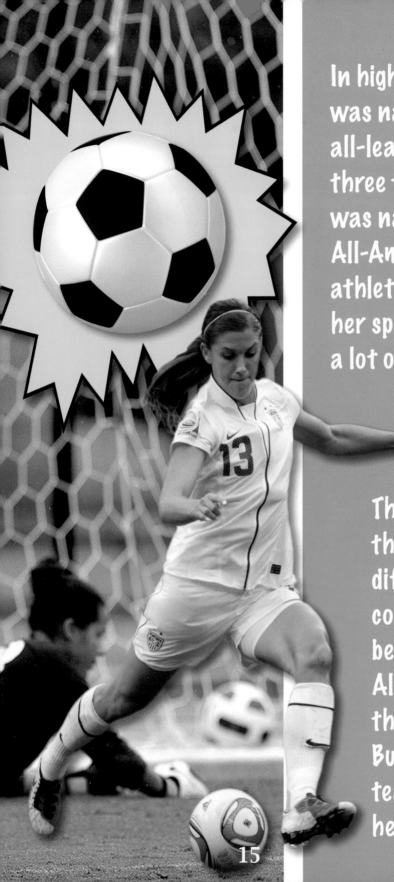

In high school she was named to the all-league team three times and was named an All-American athlete. She used her speed to score a lot of goals.

That meant that a lot of different colleges would be offering Alex a spot on their teams. But another team wanted her too.

Alex was chosen to play on the US Under-17 and then the Under-20 Women's National Teams. Players from these teams often go on to play for the Senior US Women's National soccer team.

COACH TONY DICICCO

While she was scoring goals against players from all over the world, Alex also starred for her college team. She had decided to study and play soccer at the University of California at Berkeley.

She led her college team in scoring all four years she was there and she won many awards.

While she was still in college, Alex's dream came true. Even though she was only 20 years old, she became a member of

the US Women's National team. She began to play in matches against national teams from other countries around the world.

When she graduated, Alex decided to keep playing soccer. In 2011, she was the first player to be chosen by a professional team. Alex would be playing for a team called the Western New York Flash. She has also played for the Seattle Sounders and the Portland Thorns.

ALEX PLAYS FOR
THE PORTLAND THORNS

Alex played wonderfully during the 2011 World Cup tournament. She helped the United States get to the championship game, which they lost to Japan.

ALEX COMPETES AGAINST CANADA'S LAUREN SESSELMAN

Alex's best performance so far came at the 2012 Olympics in London. She scored an amazing goal in the semifinal game against Canada. Her goal put the United States in the final game, where they won the gold medal!

ALEX

In 2012, Alex was named the US Soccer Female Athlete of the Year. But she wouldn't stop at just soccer—Alex decided to become a writer, too! Her first book was published in 2013. *Saving the Team* tells the story of a smart young soccer player named Devin. When her family moves across the country to California, her life is changed forever!

ALEX WAS NOMINATED FOR THE FIFA WOMEN'S WORLD SOCCER PLAYER OF THE YEAR AWARD

THE KICKS
Saving the Team

BY OLYMPIC GOLD MEDALIST
ALEX MORGAN

In her spare time Alex likes to practice yoga, and go snowboarding and shopping.

Alex loves animals and has a cat named Brooklyn. She also helps a group called the ASPCA to stop people from hurting animals. In 2011, she raced in the Chicago Marathon to raise $5,000 for the ASPCA.

What's next for this young soccer star? Alex and her American teammates are getting ready to play in the 2014 World Cup and the 2016 Summer Olympics. Both will be held in Brazil.

Alex has accomplished things she could only dream of as a child. Now she wants to help other girls reach their dreams! She says she will hold a soccer camp in Southern California to teach young girls what she's learned. Alex hopes to see girls being given more chances to play sports. As she told the *Los Angeles Times,* "Now it's our responsibility to help grow the game."

ALEX SIGNS
AUTOGRAPHS

31

FURTHER READING

BOOKS

Morgan, Alex. *Saving the Team*. New York: Simon & Schuster, 2013.

ON THE INTERNET

Biography.com: "Alex Morgan"
http://www.biography.com/people/alex-morgan-20837393

The Official Website of Alex Morgan
http://www.alexmorgansoccer.com/

US Soccer: "Alex Morgan"
http://www.ussoccer.com/teams/wnt/m/alex-morgan.aspx

WORKS CONSULTED

Baxter, Kevin. "Soccer Star Alex Morgan Leads a Model Life." *Los Angeles Times*, September 16, 2012. http://articles.latimes.com/2012/sep/16/sports/la-sp-0916-alex-morgan-20120916

Borden, Sam. "Rising as Fast as Her Feet Will Take Her." *The New York Times*, July 22, 2012. http://www.nytimes.com/2012/07/23/sports/olympics/alex-morgan-rising-as-fast-as-her-feet-will-take-her.html?pagewanted=all

Foss, Mike. "Alex Morgan Talks Olympics, Colbert, and Swimsuit Edition." *USA Today*, July 2, 2012. http://content.usatoday.com/communities/gameon/post/2012/07/alex-morgan-talks-olympics-stephen-colbert-and-swimsuit-edition/1#.Uf2xkY-3vuSp

The Official Website of Alex Morgan. http://www.alexmorgansoccer.com/

Roenigk, Alyssa. "Alex Morgan Makes Most of Moment." ESPN.com, August 7, 2012. http://espn.go.com/los-angeles/story/_/id/8241637/2012-summer-olympics-alex-morgan-makes-most-olympic-moment

US Soccer. "Alex Morgan." http://www.ussoccer.com/teams/wnt/m/alex-morgan.aspx

US Soccer. "Alex Morgan Accepts the US Soccer 2012 Female Athlete of the Year Award." December 4, 2012. http://www.ussoccer.com/media-library/videos/us-women/2012/12/alex-morgan-accepts-the-u-s--soccer-201-female-athlete-of-the-year-award.aspx

US Soccer. "What's In a Name?" April 4, 2013. http://www.ussoccer.com/News/Womens-National-Team/2013/04/Nicknames.aspx

INDEX

ASPCA 26
"Baby Horse" 11
Brazil 29
Chicago Marathon 26, 27
Diamond Bar, California 12
Diamond Bar High School 12–15
DiCicco, Tony 16
London 23
Morgan, Alex
  birth 12
  cat 26
  childhood 8
  college 15, 18, 20, 21
  high school 12, 15
  shopping 26
  snowboarding 26
  yoga 26
Morgan, Jennifer (sister) 12
Morgan, Jeri (sister) 12
Morgan, Michael (father) 12
Morgan, Pamela (mother) 12
Olympics 7, 23, 29
Portland Thorns 21
Saving the Team 24–25
Seattle Sounders 21
Sesselman, Lauren 23
Solo, Hope 27
University of California at Berkeley 18, 20, 21
US Soccer Female Athlete of the Year 24
US Under-17 Women's National Team 16
US Under-20 Women's National Team 16
US Women's National Team 20
Western New York Flash 21
World Cup 7, 9, 17, 22, 29